They Became Wing Perfect and Flew

Also by Toni Thomas:

Chosen
        Brick Road Poetry Press
Fast as Lightening
        Gribble Press
Walking on Water
        Finishing Line Press
Blue Halo
        Annalese Press
Ace Raider of the Unfathomable Universe
        Annalese Press
You'll be Fast as Lightning Coveting my Painted Tail
        Annalese Press
Hotsy Totsy Ballroom
        Annalese Press
Love Adrift in the City of Stars
        Annalese Press
In the Pink Arms of the City
        Annalese Press
In the Kingdom of Longing
        Annalese Press
The Things We Don't Know
        Annalese Press
In the Boarding House for Unclaimed Girls
        Annalese Press
Unburdened Kisses
        Annalese Press

They Became Wing Perfect and Flew

Poems

First published in 2022 by
Annalese Press
134 Towngate
Netherthong
Holmfirth
West Yorkshire HD9 3XZ
England

Copyright © 2022 Toni Thomas

Please Note:
All characters and situations appearing
in these pages are in the service of poetry.
Any resemblance to real persons,
living or dead, is purely coincidental.

All rights reserved. No part of this publication may be reproduced, stored, or transmitted in any form, or by any means electronic, mechanical or photo-copying, recording or otherwise, without the express written permission of the publisher.

Landscape at Pouldu, 1889-90
by Meyer Isaac de Haan
Portland Art Museum
Cover design and sketches by
Peter Wadsworth

British Library Cataloguing-in-Publication Data
A catalogue record for this book is available on request from the British Library.

Contents

PART ONE: *The Pleurisy of Wax*

I cupped a bird	3
Back then	4
Your voice is fragile bread	5
We are waltzing	6
You flirt with the bus driver	7
One day the sky wore a hole	8
You curlicue your words	9
The courtyard empties	10
The day after I married you	11
They play hide and seek	13
All night our colicky child	14
She has her Chicken Little suit on	16
Sometimes I wonder	17
I want to resist	18
I press sheets	19
We stole kisses	20

PART TWO: *The Longevity of Kisses*

I like when the morning light	25
Every day the burden of love	26
When I walk past the stone wall	27
Some places are a testament to perilous	28
The light has turned lean	29
Not every day	30
Do lovers who worship each other	31
What do the tides say	32
When I turn the pages of the dark	33

PART THREE: *Not Every Crucifix is a Bloodbath*

The day is being counted in fives	37
My father is the Earl of Misfits	38
I left early yesterday	39
One day the cut glass	40
Perhaps	41
I clipped the line in half	42
It is easy to weed	43
I am scooping up the residue	44
Some toes are pigeon pointed	45
The webbed fantasies of the dark	46
Every night does the dark	47
Some days the table talk annoys	48
When the night grew dim	49
Were there people who sailed away	50
Back then we could sing in the dark	51
Call me your diehard servant	52
I want to apologize	53
You toss my nightgowns, shampoo	54
Some of us	55

PART FOUR: *An Angel in Wait*

I want to disrobe winter	59
Past the chickweed, sport panniers	60
Some years are the years of loss	61
Among the ripple of stone houses	62
Back then were we analogs	63
I boxed the toys	64
When the hours of light dwindled	65
Pried from the pleurisy of wax	66

I shimmy into auburn curls	67
I passed you in the city today	68
Why should I curse my life	69
The little dress hanging in the window	70
It frightened me	72
You are moonlight	73
When name calling	74
Perhaps everything spills	75
Happiness called today	76
I curved my tongue	77
And have I saved the best	79

PART FIVE: *The Day of the Waltzing*

Red potatoes twirl	83
Beyond the disrobed window	84
I go around in crooked shoes	85
Past the cemetery	86
Over time	87
You wander the street	88
Beyond the huddle	89
All night	90
Every Saturday	91
Do you remember	92

*As if suddenly the roots I had left behind
cried out to me, the land I had lost with my childhood—
and I stopped, wounded by the wandering scent.*

Pablo Neruda

There was a time when people used to walk around singing

Toni Morrison

PART ONE

The Pleurisy of Wax

I cupped a bird

wanted to believe she was mine
had an affinity for light
southern places.

All morning the salt stings
the ocean grows restless.
I remember you in your white shirt
shadowed by poplar
Rilke stalled on your lips
remember the truculent of you
the welcome home
goodbyes.

A starling nested in my hand
for a few minutes I wanted
to imagine she was mine
fine feathered, red crested
small but sturdy

wanted to imagine things don't bust
a girl can remain rustproof

that up the road
you walk towards me
with a brisk gait
spell my name
as homecoming
song.

Back then

I buttoned my cardigan loose
swore by a festive moon, puppets
helped you plant rhubarb, carrots, cabbage.
The chiffon of my mother's dress
spoke more than civil.

Back then the wind traveled the earth
without mocking
I folded paper planes
launched them through the air
in search of your heart.

The kitchen smelt of Italian plums.
You sliced their bodies diligent
laid them out neat and flat
as a tribe of nuns
instructed me to follow instructions
brush light with butter.

I sang *Lo How a Rose E'er Blooming*
promised to be faithful.
Would this be enough?

Your voice is fragile bread

in a heat factory
    all morning the pavement steams
        our parrot garden empties
    wool socks, a stippled hanky
        wait under the bed.

I remember that December
    of snowdrifts
        the cheap flight to Prague
    nights of borsht, monkfish
        your voice lifting slow
            as a well ordered sail

my spike heels spilt across carpet
    what gets handpicked
        saved
            turns perilous.

We are waltzing

Mind my toes
carefully prescribed angles
home tour
bright foliage.

But you are not the friend
who listens

gargantuan want
till I am shirtless
till the python smirks
then swallows.

Cut glass and blood spill.

See how stereophonic
the future leans
the past gives up its landmines

how out of the slant
corner of your eye
my wounded bird sings.

You flirt with the bus driver

not me
blow kisses into private emails
disguise your cramped lover
in a makeshift

anchor to abstract sunset
blue neon, textbooks.

Back then I wanted space
not distance
room to breathe
then a tango.

One day the sky wore a hole

nothing could fill
the sun stayed indoors
cowered
some called it famine
some called it a nasty trick
of the dark's lurid sister.

Crops grew thin
ants vanished
the grass turned languid.

Is it hard to lure things back
know what to do -
be more than a shopkeeper's bread sale
invalid moon in need of a friend?

You curlicue your words

salt them till they resemble french fries
tossed into red ketchup
nibbled along the boardwalk.

I come upon *nefarious*
double-bind, infantile morning
co-dependent rammed up
against *suffragette longing*
success object and *selfish*
the words are greasy, hard to eat
slip from my hands
like tainted fish.

You curlicue your words
speculative marries *strategic*
your needs wedded to *adultery*.

Over time I become incredulous
how you can plug a drain
stab the dark
vandalize

bleed the heart dry
with such fat rhetoric.

The courtyard empties

our gerbil waits in her cage
summer magazines with bikinied blondes
infest the coffee table.
You practice sedition
brilliant similes
practice maybe and forever.

Am I waiting on the message
that never comes
the durable one
not vanilla trapped in a snow cone?

Over time you amp up the stakes
coin our love a *time bomb*
sex den   gutted kitchen
as if no one kicks in the door
breaks a woman's nose
serializes love into a travelling suitcase.

Is there virtue in waiting
not turning patience into a cue ball?

The day after I married you

the wind rose fierce
a damp mist gloomed our yard
the acorn squash slumped
under October's grey maul.

At the pump house
we undammed wet leaves
took the trail bordered by clear-cuts
past blackberry bushes dangling
the last of their pocked fruit.

Who would not be happy in an hour
on a day like this one
the neighbor's horse truant in the field
my black lab tracing our steps as she sniffed
the wind insistent but not spiteful
the promise of molten lovemaking
sweet potato stew on the stove

why wouldn't I believe nothing dries up
cannot be conquered
by our newly claimed thirst
that the festive peonies
propped in my kitchen vase
speak of more than obduracy
are opal wings, the bright flange
of a joyous future

why wouldn't I believe
that the path to the spring stays true
will always welcome our twined bodies
with the splash of snowbells?

They play hide and seek

are married to balmy weather
park space, tree hide
voices that blare a trumpet
school a whisper

are five and eight
in love with frog slippers
flashlights, sneaky card games
sleepovers

every roadmap steams
their name.

They are young pups
ready and willing
night angels protect
lovers kiss

nobody bludgeons a cat
strategizes divorce
snaps the house in two.

All night our colicky child

won't sleep sound
is up for water, a kiss, biscuit, moon song
as if settling down is a death sentence.

And I remember back then
how I never settled down
waited up hours
after the children were bedded

remember those forays
the 2am of me in my short negligee
traveling the corridors of the house
down to the basement
where you'd sit typing those private emails
the bottle of red wine
my soft soothes then cry fits
pleas for you to stop
come back upstairs

how you'd grin
kiss me on the forehead
tell me the emails to other women
my brunette boss
are mere fiction
don't jeopardize the marriage
kiss me perfunctory
the way we dismiss an unruly child
wave away winter

how you could exit a hug, a bed
a marriage
make believe you were still present
never culpable.

She has her Chicken Little suit on

the one that albums the world
allows you to lie
about the state of the heart
the nation
who will/will not commit adultery
die a forlorn death.
It makes for avoidance
forensic nights
an ambassadorship of shopkeepers.

In the kitchen off Malden Road
a woman implores *please be faithful*
your dinner of mashed potato, pork chop
waits on the stove.

She has her Chicken Little suit on.
Out the window taxis blare
the night traffics in secrets.

Sometimes I wonder

if the hanging of clothes saves
if I tote your socks, boxer shorts

cream shirts out to hang
in the sun cured yard

you'll talc my loyalty
ability to calm and not chaff

later slip into slacks, a dress coat
carry the scent of my hands

not as thin branches that break
but the faith of baskets that carry

load after load
sudsed
rinsed out, hauled

sanctified
in your name.

I want to resist

school my lips to forget
the easy *yes*
rise up against the fashionable
words hermetically sealed
in a glass jar.

No I will not genuflect to celebrity
suffer a false note
no I am not perfect
a debutante, dilettante, mock emblem
no the world is not doing well
animals disappear
people suffer

I will no longer say it your way
just because.

I want to resist
coax my voice into more
than false bravado
punctuated caviar.

I press sheets

press, press, press
till they are smooth
and the world sings.

In the kitchen pudding and mint tea
in the yard a spotted dog
spotted past
buried in basalt.

It is October
no one expects paradise
a sundress, Jesus sandals

the weather weeps then dries up
the man you love turns vagrant
you give him room
give him room.

There are lunchboxes
pajamas with little feet
clothes that refuse to dry
on the yard line.

In the kitchen
Ella crones *the man I love*
I want to stumble back
into singing.

We Stole Kisses

They were wind and April
meant for another couple
but we were young, brazen

believed the world has short corridors
a surfeit of cake
that the river calls our name
our name
nothing dries up, frizzles.

We stole kisses
carried them till our backs ached
promised to be faithful
fed them mackerel and honey
tinctures of Saturn.

But time mistresses the dark
with its own blue trajectory
flip flops words
ices the face
turns suitcases heavy.

First we stole kisses
then you stole the moon
my morning slippers, my heart
put it in a glass case
under the heat lamp
went to gather other hearts
kisses, conquests.

Tell me –
will what's been taken come back
will the girl riding in the blue rickshaw
know something about sunset
her diaphanous longing
how even unbidden
it gathers inside her

a steady flame?

PART TWO

The Longevity of Kisses

I like when the morning light

settles in after the rain
glazes the beige stone of the houses
tilted chimneys
woodbins, cobbled streets
that gaze off into the distance.

Maybe we could reclaim our lives
in a place like this
start slow as if no one
really knows us
past the lovesick nights
carefully prescribed paintwork
small lies meant to console

could wake up
a different voice
be more than hard flint
half spent kisses
watch the birds move
field to tree to house
rise up once and for all

singing.

Every day the burden of love

invades me
your sickled trellises
weighed suitcase.
I borrow hope
from the landlord
live on borsht
a coal fire
poems

as if even the cold
snowfield
wind blinded birds
hold more than mercantile
are roads that travel me

candle and bread
bright ember
secret word.

When I walk past the stone wall

shrouded in ivy, enter your metal gate
the tombstones stay pensive
don't set up a welcome party
wave

and even the silver birch
almost skeletal now
barely quivers
stays respectful of the dead
the secrets we carry

as if peace is wordless
and any passersby winded
from the steep climb up the hill
can clamber into this shade
become vestige
psalm.

When I walk past the stone wall
enter the cemetery
the headstones don't rattle
make a riotous big deal
rinse their voice of debris
angle a new face, peep show
complain about neglect

but still their spirits carry me
invite
as if life never truly empties.

Some places are a testament to perilous

walk a shaky road
lip read loss
turn dismissed landscape
empty shop, lease sign.

I clip food coupons
read the sales copy on detergent
watch the neighbor girl cradle her rag doll
the green grocer bag potato, carrots
the hardware man cut keys
watch boot soles get mended
the second hand bookseller
reshelf his fiction.

There are roadways that sustain
keep loss from wrecking
goodness we can't manufacture
that hallows the soul.

The light has turned lean

walks on tiptoe
but not my heart
its sodden and risky
that ambles along the dirt path
mud, rock, field
down to town
where the butcher bags pork chops
bread shelves empty
arugula sits loose in wood bins.

What do I know of endurance
the peephole pressed to the wind
that stays stalwart
handholds the past
how the curio shop of the heart
can remain nimble
your vixen claim?

Not every day

holds an avenue of uninterrupted light
where children play
rooms stay decent
testify to the longevity of a kiss
to bookshelves, tallboys, sofas
where entwined bodies spell out
the vocabulary of their lovemaking.

Were you once in love?
What did it feel like?

More than words
more than acrimony
tall ships eclipsing a shallow sunrise

I want to see you rise up
not holding the world
in a vice grip
but soft.

Do lovers who worship each other

throw fate to the wind
make love on fire escapes
the bridge of Japanese gardens
conjure starlight
an unburdened trajectory of kisses

do they wake early
unravel the bed
parade in kangaroo pajamas
pine scented cologne

wax prophetic
rekindle their first lovemaking
harbor pigeons and swallows
a secret language for gift

will their luck hold out
roots stay strong
will there be rainy Sundays
play fights and popcorn
corny jokes, crushes of ice cream

do lovers who worship each other
stall the future
feed it good bread, honey

keep an easy pace
as if the press of their bodies
is deeper than ruin
wider than leave-taking?

What do the tides say

about moon embalmed nights
muscled sea merchants
the woman who dips her body
half off the pleasure boat
and drowns

what do the tides say
about gull feather
green algae, whales breaching
campfires and red toxin

will they soft sooth a child
wash up the condemned ice box
navigate loss
drift unmanned as a loose skiff?

What causes them to stay faithful
generous
a world beyond shipwreck?

When I turn the pages of the dark

tempt in my slinkiest dress
imagine the night spangled
the easy suitor
my name gladly engraved
on the face of your cake

when I turn the pages of the dark
is it best to place complicated words
in a zip bag
find the least ferocious homily
arrived empty?

PART THREE

Not Every Crucifix is a Bloodbath

The day is being counted in fives

then in twenty-fours
till all hours are assigned
nothing gets lost
we can sleep in a smoothed bed
inside crisp sheets, a moon lamp.

No one wants to act with impertinence
feudal the land
take more than their share
bank it

but still the world has its compartments
prescribed season for oyster
lunchboxes
shined shoes
subways
the lit up computer face
bar bells and zumba

our surplus attempts
at lovemaking.

My father is the Earl of Misfits

that Canterbury forgot
keeps his wounded blue boy heart
in his waistcoat
staples mountains
turns the sea into a backwater.

All my life I have bowed at his feet
tossed away privilege
fed kumquats to his pit-bull
hoped for favor, good grace

fell in love with a man who shadows him
wears demand like a sodden prince
never weeps
green folios the house
expects spotless rhetoric
no nonsense.

My father is the mighty Earl of Misfits.
You can see him in my lover's face
the pale taut skin, dismissals
the way he calculates misfortune
turns every childlike step
into a fallen clause
debauchery.

I left early yesterday

do you remember
the day you said the word divorce
started tearing up the house
slipped off your coat
transferred the rain.

Now I am a field of rain
it seeps into my body
slicks down my hair
keeps my lips from faulty.

My daughter treads gently
knows the price of absence
a blue orphanage
the way the night burns
red firmament
a blind moon.

One day the cut glass

and bulletproof were not enough
fur fell from the animals
children hushed
the rooms turned faceless.

Inside the gutter weeds fingered
matter of fact you said *I am divorcing you*
a storage locker was rented
the night became armed with pistols.

Later as the children slept
you broke down the door
I'd latched to our bedroom
insisted it is *your room, your bed*

that no matter what
nobody is about to get up
on their high horse
start denying you.

Perhaps

it was not always shrill cold
periled chocolate
not always the icy voice
my mother's body preserved in aspic
the winter birds ripped from her tree.

I have little recollection
how we persevered
made potato into a four way casserole
sewed stamina into our coat sleeves

but still winter descended
the night dragged its feet guttural
our bodies became strangers
someone wound the dark into a play toy
you sang the *Bride of Penzance*
buried our marriage.

I clipped the line in half

decapitated its head
clean washbasin
no bloodbath
snip snip
anointed it with a loin cloth
fig tree, acrimony
a voice box of useful amends.

You wink
debate the night angel
practice robotics
are muscular, streamlined
abhor the imposition of commas
to an end game.

I clipped you in half
made room for breath
colored pantomimes
floozy rhetoric
the unkempt grass
beyond mercury.

It is easy to weed

yank things out till they perish
never commit disorder
the unsightly
over our lawn's future.

Sometimes we yank hair
lovers, jobs, a place, family
out of our life
as if they are cankers
wave to them
in their deathbed.

I have a mother who waved goodbye
to her paintings, her appetite, her life
became a maimed heart
with no future.

Some gardens are time bombs
their mission is to detonate
they take the birds, the blue sky
doll's house

leave us with thunder
then a terrible calm.

I am scooping up the residue

of the marriage
tidy the storage locker
its implicit and referential
the names for my things plastered with
your black marker on the cardboard boxes –
*Bedroom. Anna's office. Bathroom Things.
Anna's poetry books. Miscellaneous.*

Does it make you feel smart, capable
sweeping the family house clean
exiting the mother
will you go on to sleep well in your bed
with my boss, the other woman
mind the children
be a different kind of lover

quit the porn, red river
stop making every around the corner
next in line
your prey?

Some toes are pigeon pointed

they may not have started out that way
but the rain came
and it was never vanilla.

If we sweep a life clean
will it admit its nosegays
pardon the past for cramped rooms
brown scissors?

Some days the rain weeps.
Call it a blue cleansing.
Call it my heart's leakage.

Don't tell me to button up
empire your actions
when inside me ribbons a river.
It is strong and fierce
breaks through barriers

travels your trash heap
the torn pinwheels
you've chained in my
watchtower.

The webbed fantasies of the dark

do not lie flat
will get up on hind legs
beg for their supper
turn the body into a sphinx or siren
capture a shrunken life
squeeze.

At one time I thought daydreams
were imagination's meadow
could riot the room
pinch a bird to sing
eat with no muzzle.

The webbed fantasies of the dark
wear high heels, boot spurs
set up their own voice box
will memorize money then spit
tell you what you can and can't do
leave you on an iced bridge
in a faux fur coat
half naked
wordless.

Every night does the dark

cast out ordinary straw
look for pound notes
a mercenary pursuit

set up a bank account
for falcons
constellations of stars so thirsty
they carpetbag
quarrel over whether the roof
should be thrown in as
expense column or asset

every night does the dark
cast dice rolls
win/lose
as if the world is up for grabs
we are pinned to prize money
a racecourse?

My daughter anchors down
her favorite stuffed animals
hides the doll house
blue Wedgewood tea service
just in case.

Some days the table talk annoys

vanilla bean with no edge
shiny train with a vacant face.
I twirl my green beans around
sink them in the pool of cheese.

Some days are no picnic
the sun refuses the sky
the woman in her pale shift
disavows insolence
sits deterred in a breadbox.

I have spent years learning to spell.
There is an art to this
like lovemaking
the ceremony of castoffs.

In your presence it is not difficult
to feel like a castoff
blue orphanage.

Do you know the facts of love?
Are you sure?

When the night grew dim

homilies shriveled
when my mother sang for bread
that would never be hers
still you mounted the stairs
to my heart
waited.

I was fifteen
knew little about promises
good that is surplus
to the world's needs

knew little about death
the way it takes
what we receive
the shrill note of clipped orchids

how a being can mount your stair
in a different voice
come back.

Were there people who sailed away

never came back
called by the sea into the
liquid composure of selkies

and what will you say of me then
when I refind the skin
that was peeled from me
wriggle into it
slide back into the dark water
that waits loyal mistress
across my landlocked days
my children's birth ground
the men who mired me with kisses
that blessed as they fled

and what will you say
when the waves conquer
the house sits empty
the linen folded
my blue dress splayed across the floor
the hob still warm from the tin of scones

what will you do when my love notes
scatter about the bed
and the poems, hundreds of them
and the knowledge I was never
a permanent fixture
landlocked, incurable

where will you go
what will become of you?

Back then we could sing in the dark

mouth parenthetical morning
a pipe organ, toy monkey
savior the world with our words
as if seed pods succor
the spilt hand bespeaks
an unfrosted heart.

Are there still nights
inherited moments
when the clock refrains
the skin of the building peels
periled apples are worth more
than a pipe dream?

In the slate house lives a girl
who moves past acrimony
your careless orchard
waits prostrate
a remainder of wings.

Call me your diehard servant

crippled girl on a blind limb
decanter of nothing
pie in the sky diadem

suck out the juice
litter my yard
harpoon the hairballs
empty vagrant my past
till it is ragged cotton

rest me in the pale season
of your shaved haberdashery

but remember
every drowned house
in the final notice
holds a reserve
season to tell.

I want to apologize

mother forgive us
our malnutrition
foibles that are black tar
malaria

forgive us this dose of vice
that lives in vinegar

as if the everlasting repairs

even in America
love can absolve bruises
last.

You toss my nightgowns, shampoo

hairbrush, coat, shoes, books
into cardboard boxes
shove them in a storage locker
two miles down the road

erase picture albums
a family, wife

wipe your hands clean
the catholic academic
selfless.

I cast my lot
into the world
suffer the losses
relearn it is good.

Some of us

wander the shore
as smoked vanilla
no ordinary headset.

You took the moat
toy spade, turrets
spent what you please
cast weight into a dustbin
littered your plantation
with pestilence
mangroves.

But little known to the trajectory
of lawless
there are other filigrees
women at night with no clothes
a faithless husband
who turn themselves
into more than bedrock.

They flame.

PART FOUR

An Angel in Wait

I want to disrobe winter

find the note that saves
hawk my body
in and out of your flame

as if a room waits
that is more than thin light
the fluid verse turned sump hole

keep faith
there is power
in the night's mischief

no dark, pithy angel
is more arresting
than an angel in wait.

Past the chickweed, sport panniers

street litter of kittens
corner vendor serving pad thai
past leggy vows, a strip show
the woman breathing fire for a coin

past poltergeists
Fannie with her entourage of suitors
tarot cards that cargo the future for a kiss
past roasted lamb on the spit
crayons that crown purple over concrete

past our hopes, maybes
mornings of soapstone and light
gossip and coffee
past anonymous rooms
people weeping

past all of this
there waits a light
that does not dye its words yellow
need to swap place
set up a pay day
lives in the oil skin, the sponge cake
the groats and the kiln
the tantric cross
comes to me day and night
is more than a nameplate, stopgap
quick fix, blue oasis
stores rice for my wedding day

sings and delivers
sings and delivers.

Some years are the years of loss

so thick
words turn blue razor
painted puppets
secretly cull the herd
behead the obsolete woman.

I have come away with a leery sense
of what's possible
what is truth
have come away with my life
a slow restitution
homecoming.

Listen – when the sky falls in
don't expect men to save you.
There will be dark nights
an empty bread basket
inns with no room
your children will curse the cruel
hand they've been dealt
pin blame on the nameless.

You will sit in a room
examine god, loss, faith.
But, my friend, wait past that day
and the next
even longer
for the sky does not armor the moon
exile the sun forever.

Spring comes.
It comes.
Make ready for her eventual nosegays.

Among the ripple of stone houses

that ride up the cobbled street
with their late spilt roses
blackened chimneys dusted with starlings
rowan splash against the September sky.

And how many times in my life have I yearned
for something just beyond my reach
as if the roof tile
footed pajamas pinned to the clothesline
pudding and roast
worn stones, cow pasture
mud strewn path
were only a runt road
in a sea of snatched eggs.

Today there are starlings chattering.
The sun has returned
steadies itself across the valley
and one double rainbow momentarily
climbs the distance.
You tell me it means a pot of gold
somewhere out there in the pasture.
But I am not looking for pots of gold
only this.

Back then were we analogs

of bright wing
almsgiving
tinctures and Saturn

did we chronicle the grass
prophetic
travel well in our shoes
did our voices come over as
more than beggarly

were we pileated tulle
woodpecker, plover
could we jezebel the past
file away its deathbeds?

Spring is impish
arrives with elfin feet
a nosegay
keeps lovers safe.

In her whisper
even the sharp wind
turns deft curve
comprehensible.

I boxed the toys

pale throated mourning
slipped into brown shoes
a cardboard house

till slowly, very slowly
the emerald gifts of March appeared
the variegated woodpecker
forsythia, spilt purple of crocus

and over time I have become
more than speechless

learned to seed the garden
with my own voice.

When the hours of light dwindled

I stumbled
amid cut glass
shrunken architects
plastic

but that was years ago
when the waters shrank
the forest was torn
from its rosebuds.

Over time
when the light grew back
the sky no longer leaked

I called out your name
its beauty and terror
blood and pathos

fed you bird seed
orange
whispered *holy*

till the sea of my heart
stopped leaking
emptiness
grew a nest egg.

Pried from the pleurisy of wax

I stomp my feet
crayon the snow
hide in trees
dog language

cauterize loss
to keep the sky
from falling

nest your moon
in my lap
palpable.

I shimmy into auburn curls

a bang set
mini skirt, mud boots
no chicken little
with a deferred flame

lick the past into crystal
melt men
pole-vault over buildings
sully the contrived map work
watch you burn
beyond crop shares

high wire roof to tree
tree to pole
as if we stand for something.

The earth reigns.

I passed you in the city today

pretended we were strangers
that you had never run for office
in the suitcase of my heart

remember home
a child's bake oven
furry cat slippers
the bruise marks
fabric of loss
that over time turned bright
as a war trophy.

Out in the street
cranes fly low
love dusts the back of strangers
a woman's wet lips

a paper parrot flies on a stick
rice lands on foreheads
the blue stroller
scalloped hedge
reminds me of snow
a wedding ceremony
blossoms of pear tree.

Why should I curse life

create a blue talisman
hold it up to the glass cube
make it dance for meals
like a trained monkey?

Despite our forgetfulness
the earth gives
offers up her jewels
acorn and snowfield
wet meadow
blue gentian
deer, elk, coyote
the tall summer grass swaying

just this once – to be in them
consumed.

The earth yields.

My palm cups
remnant of spring
tadpole, moss, burdock
river, bridge
ancient gift giving.

The little dress hanging in the window

of the house across the river in the reformed stone mill
could be the dress of the child I aborted years ago
when the man I loved insisted inconvenience
badgered day after day that the timing was wrong
we can't do this
that he had a novel to write
years ago when my mother had just died
and my father was far away with the crisp new fiancé

the round collared dress could belong to
the young girl who lodges in my heart
wet as a rainy day
terrible sadness
the fledgling dream to grow into someone
that was never to be -
lack of money, lack of family, a probationary lover
can do something

is the reason I will lobby nine years later to adopt
the oldest girl stranded in an orphanage
eddy my way into that boat, transatlantic journey
want her to know simple dresses like this one
be the reclaimed bride
the one never forgotten
sister to my own son.

The little dress hanging in the window
could be the one my daughter learns to dance in
could fit on the girl who has grown up
in my heart's rear view mirror
the one I barely know

the one who scratched, implored in her rag coat
begged and bargained against his voice's straightjacket
my fears, the icy reprimands
till on a steel-eyed lonely day in August

she slid away
but I promised never to forget.

The little dress hanging in the window
of the house in the reclaimed mill
could be the same dress my four-year-old daughter
will receive when I arrive across an ocean
to the orphanage in Guangzhou
her body screwed into a pelted football sweat suit
birthmark on her back spread winged as the butterfly
bald spot on her short cropped hair
as she holds one paper bag with wrapped candy
the only possession she will carry away
wonders why it took so long to reach her

and I will not tell her about treacherous seas
the man in a spotted raincoat
jittery plight of the moon to keep the night solvent
only how sometimes it takes a lifetime
to learn how to navigate
make our dreams oasis
that life is precious
hope asks us to believe
what is erased can grow back
unmanned in the heart's suitcase.

It frightened me

the tumult of noise
reckless flutter of leaves
before the rooks fell from the tree
quickly regained enough poise
to not hit the ground
became wing perfect and flew.

Is this what passion does
this unmitigated free fall
the loss of north/south
east/west
as if we can defy gravity
our past
shake the future
as if death maims no country
every mooring is palpable.

And will I stumble heedless then
into this dark wet room
give up my will
preeminence
the practiced job, boxed yard
let my stammer slide into kisses
peck you speechless
in the bright knowledge
our greatest riches
are already here?

You are moonlight

and white thighs
skin smooth
unmangled as the river

come from the north country
up past Edinburgh
where sheep graze
wash flaps wild on clotheslines
winter snow blinds the field.

It is hard to know
if the sky listens
I will live in more than the
salvation of poems

sleep inside
the bright highway
yellow lamp
of your gaze.

When name calling

became a thing of the past
the sun sat rusted
I embroidered a new kind of field
armed it with rice
nosegays
the Almond River

armed it with kitty call girls
becalmed soldiers
men who don't drive machines
refuse to become them

armed it with cattle cries
escaped chicken
lux of light
more than homogenous future.

See how you scatter bird seed
among the indigent
topple the sarcastic mayor
grind down lust
rake the yard

populate my dark water
with castoff kisses
stories
till the fish bite.

Perhaps everything spills

from here
the bandy chickens in the neighbor's coop
the boy with his toot whistle
cramped teeth
clothes on the line lifting
the muddy *For Sale* sign
on the shuttered house

the blue sky turned ageless
as if we are meant to stray
our bodies splayed
across loose stone
cow pasture
crevice and concrete.

Darling – stay with me then.
Let our nights be the bee's mischief
our days laden with this.

Happiness called today

said *stop wandering*
offered up a room
cook stove, bath.

Sometimes it takes just a little
to succor the heart
keep the rain from hazardous.

Happiness called
I made soup
sat at a newfound table
thanked the roof for hosting
the radiator for warmth

let your fingers spill across
my body ripe as a poem.

I curved my tongue

around wax papered french fries
till one by one they reached into
my mouth's dark chamber and sank

curled my tongue around pitted fantasies
a coined fountain, blue vapor
girlish wishes, hard candy
the seal of soft envelopes
around periscopes
things stalled in aspic
jars stabbed red with pimento

curled my tongue around cellophane
waxwork figures and surly
the child who shines shoes
poker faced landlords
eyelet pantyhose
polished midnight
the man stealing kisses as he counts

curled my tongue around foreclosure
divided families
years of single parenting Christmas
what gets traitored
what gets saved

but then you came –
matchless in your chiffon dress
cheap glitter of rhinestones
tied a sail around fantasy
and I never walked away

want to cup my tongue around
your body's white trellis
as if love still swoons, saves
with its savage and candlelit.

Out of the trials of my winter
you came whole clothe
feed me no hyssop
end games
but this.

And have I saved the best

of my love for you
not just brushed words and a zip coat
plastic corsages pinned ageless

saved the best of my love
its pine scented
that comes from the high country
wanders among deer, fox
the blind moon
young girl's missives
comes with a feathered entourage
blue swale

and will you take me places
I have never been
cure my sick ward
cup the stars
splay them across my bed
brighter than the gold in a bank vault?

PART FIVE

The Day of the Waltzing

Red potatoes twirl

genuflect in the bins
of the shop vendor
the hosed street glistens
the man who loves to nap
comes awake

whistles sound
cars jostle
traffic lights flicker with love notes

the Saturday night deaths
I once knew
have flown

what waits
comes alive
inside the heart's unburdened
barrel of mercury.

Beyond the disrobed window

the sun chars newspaper
warms ants, swallows
pavement steams
the street vendor offers up sausage
the ventriloquist rinses his voice
hay bales crisp
amber ransoms the autumn.

Beyond the disrobed window
flour sacks heave
envelopes get plastered with love notes
winged mothers rise from stone

and quietly in the nest of my ear
you sing.

I go around in crooked shoes

plant cosmos, nosegays
wet nurse the moon
make your fire escape my home.

Birds deposit their nest eggs
rocks preen
leaves tumble
the sky rehearses our voice.

In the atrium
Minerva sings
your fountain spills over
with soothsay.

Past the cemetery

the church of St. Cuthbert
the posters for Evensong
Gregorian Chant
past the Black Cat Pub
where three fiddlers are playing

past the man with the birthmark
who conceals the pale petals of his face
past the Celtic cross, hungry pigeons
the child spinning her felted bird on a string

past the blue beggar
groomed horses
riders in smart jackets, leather boots
past the outdoor cafes
plates of smoked salmon, paté

beyond the shop talk
forevers and maybes
I will meet you

clear as the candle burns
true as the cobblestones on the quay
pressed by the world's tired feet
polished over time
defenseless.

Over time

I have learned to swim in your green ocean
host a field leavened with eggs
half dozed lovers whose bluesy kisses
make the grass grow
the trees grateful.

Bright bands of hedera
scripture the house.

My teardrops
water the phlox
bluebells, sedge
keep the daisies from limpid
turn your river
into a font.

You wander the street

amid kebab vendors
meat pasties, periled flags
double decker buses
neon signs that gyrate

deal in dice roll
pinstriped suits
the poppy splashed meadow
blue hoodies
fiddle playing
carrot, sausage, bread, potato
faces soft milled as flour
red tinged with wind.

Children run sleeveless
chips get doused in vinegar
knee high boots strut, taxis gleam
strollers rattle
a toddler sucks his thumb
the sky hands out puff balls.

You seep into clotheslines
spot clean windows
handhold lovers
percolate coffee

unburden the past
of its ruinous rooms
turn my meager voice
into meadow.

Beyond the huddle

of soot stained houses
bug born fantasies
plastic bouquets for the deceased

I watch your face
that is the soft skin of custard

watch you traipse
through the slush fields
carry my cross weightless.

Everyday
we meet in this place
where whippoorwills sing
the sky slow turns its sorrow
where my callow hands
relearn sunset
let you feed and bless.

All night

the sky thirsts for nothing
stars spill
sloops lay with their dark hulls
on still as glass water
the cranium tack of the world
runs on dreamtime
rabbits riot
loaves lift
cars suck moonlight
the heart of the Jacobite uprising
is elsewhere.

All night the vigil between
life and death is wrestled
amid bed sheets
where bodies ambition
to smash distance
find a shared throne.

A forehead of light
bridles the loch
huddles the houses
keeps snug the secret vigil
of our soul's mythmaking.

Every Saturday

you light a bonfire in the square
call forth the nearly departed
the ostracized, ill bred
sing to them from a different tweed

talk about the moon's nightdress
the copper skinned snake in the field
the way sunlight succors the arms
of the poor
travels the forest

how in a certain light
certain hour of decay
everything is antique
returns to beautiful.

Do you remember

the day of the waltzing
recall my rope of hair
blue baggy dress
the jackdaws, pipers crooning
remember the pocked sun
hills burnished with autumn

and isn't it for this that the rain chants
the arms of the trees open
the cattle bless the field

that once so separate
undisclosed
we pass beyond the hour of our distance
and in the bright halo of her time
become silver glint
the morning star's faithful.

Toni Thomas lives in Portland, Oregon. Her poems have been published in Austria, Spain, New Zealand, Canada, England, Scotland, and Australia. In the United States her work has appeared in over fifty literary magazines including *Prairie Schooner, North Dakota Quarterly, Hayden's Ferry Review, the Minnesota Review, Notre Dame Review, Poetry East*, and more. She has been twice nominated for a Pushcart prize, and won several awards. She has published twelve collections of poetry and three books for children.

Her figurative clay sculptures have been shown in gallery exhibits in Portland and Chicago, displayed in literary magazines, and housed in private collections in the U.S. and England.

Her short documentary *One of Us* was shown at the Trans-ideology: Nostalgia festival in Berlin and at the Museum of
Contemporary Art in Taipei.

Since Toni loves to create and sits buried in reams of poems, manuscripts, clay figures and images….she likes to imagine all of them out in the world, swaying wild as the lupine.

tonithomaspoetry.com

www.ingramcontent.com/pod-product-compliance
Lightning Source LLC
Chambersburg PA
CBHW021444080526
44588CB00009B/679